Presented To

_____

By

_____

Date

_____

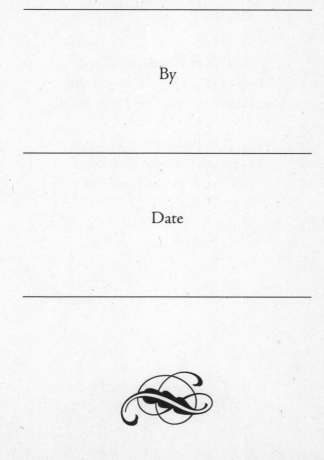

Dedication

To Don & Mardie MacLeod
Many of us are blessed as you share
your home and hospitality each holiday

To Barbara Martin
In appreciation of your critiques
and your fiction-writing skills

CHRISTMAS *Legends* TO REMEMBER

Legend of the Candy Cane
Legend of the Christmas Tree
Legend of Saint Nicholas

Helen Haidle

David C Cook®
transforming lives together

CHRISTMAS LEGENDS TO REMEMBER
Published by Honor Books®, an imprint of
David C. Cook
4050 Lee Vance View
Colorado Springs, CO 80918 U.S.A.

David C. Cook Distribution Canada
55 Woodslee Avenue, Paris, Ontario, Canada N3L 3E5

David C. Cook U.K., Kingsway Communications
Eastbourne, East Sussex BN23 6NT, England

David C. Cook and the graphic circle C logo
are registered trademarks of Cook Communications Ministries.

All Scripture quotations are taken from *The New King James Version* (NKJV).
Copyright © 1979, 1980, 1982, 1994, Thomas Nelson, Inc.

ISBN 978-1-56292-534-5

© 2002 Helen Haidle

Cover Jacket Design: Koechel Peterson & Associates, Inc., Mpls. MN

Printed in the United States of America
First Edition 2007

4 5 6 7 8 9 10 11 12 13 14

050508

Contents

Introduction

"Legend of the Candy Cane" began in 1995 when I purchased a box of candy canes. The back of the box explained the Christian symbolism hidden in the candy's shape, color, and stripes. I gave candy canes to my Sunday school students and let them practice explaining its meaning. The children took extra candy canes home to share. The next Sunday, they reported how they had shared the candy's meaning with their neighbors, classmates, and even with playground bullies.

At lunch I told my husband, "The candy cane is a unique way for kids to show and tell the message of Christmas."

He nodded. "Someone should write a story about the candy."

I nearly choked on my salad—was God nudging me to write a story about the candy cane?

Since we know little of the candy's origin, I created a story about an elderly candymaker who found hope and encouragement in an unexpected way. The story has been expanded here, centering on the candymaker and his desire to create a very special Christmas gift for his granddaughter and all the village children.

"Legend of the Christmas Tree" is derived from an old legend from Sicily. The little tree reminds us that "the Son of Man did not come to be served, but to serve" (Matthew 20:28). As I wove a tender tale about this gentle and humble tree, God's acceptance of the little tree brought a lump to my throat. It's my favorite story of all the ones I've written.

In the many stories concerning Saint Nicholas, two simple but profound elements of Christmas have emerged: giving and forgiving. The unselfish generosity of Nicholas, his firm faith, and his willingness to return good for evil remind us of timeless Christmas truths in "Legend of Saint Nicholas."

May these three legends reaffirm anew God's great love, mercy, and faithfulness during this Christmas season.

—Helen Haidle

Legend of the Candy Cane

A New Day of Faith

Many years ago on a wintry morning, a warm light glowed through the frosty windows of a candy shop. Martin Winckler, an elderly gentleman in his 80s, shuffled past the large glass case filled with jars of colored candies. He unlocked the front door, hung an OPEN sign in its frosted window, and silently gazed outside at the village street.

A blanket of fresh snow covered the road, lampposts, and roofs of every small

Jesus said to him, "If you can believe, all things are possible to him who believes."
MARK 9:23

shop along the street, making the snowy village look like a picture postcard.

Standing inside, the candymaker listened to the approaching sounds of jingling bells as people drove their horse-drawn sleighs to work. The music echoed cheerfully through the dark streets.

But no answering notes of joy echoed in the old man's heart. He blinked the unformed tears from his eyes and turned away from his decorated front door. Sighing deeply, he turned his attention to the pot-bellied stove near the front of his shop.

He bent down slowly onto one knee, pulled open the stove door, and stirred the coals. Reaching into the bucket next to the stove, he lifted out several logs and added them to the flickering fire. After he closed the door, he paused to pet the striped tabby cat at his knee.

"Yes, Sebastian. You appreciate a warm fire too, don't you?" He sighed again and scratched Sebastian's chin and neck. "Ah, my faithful friend. I only wish you could talk to me once in a while. Maybe you know how difficult it is for me to get ready for Christmas—

a Christmas without my Katherine. And now it's time for me to do the one job I've been dreading since her death. I don't want to, but I have to—for the sake of the children—and for my own sake too." Sebastian purred and rubbed his face against Martin's leg.

Martin stood up slowly, gingerly. *Life must go on,* he thought, *even when it seems impossible. It's what she would want me to do.* But setting up the Christmas manger scene had always been Katherine's job, her special delight. Each time he thought of setting it up, in his mind's eye Martin would see Katherine placing each figure just so with her loving hands as she chatted gaily about their Christmas plans. How he prayed for the ache of her absence to subside a little. Yet it remained—heavy as a load of bricks. One moment she had been with him—the next she was gone. The reality of her absence still didn't seem possible.

Reluctantly, Martin walked over to the bottom shelf of the cupboard, pulled out an old wooden chest, and carried it to the shop window. Katherine had already decorated the window with fragrant pine boughs and red garlands, not knowing she wouldn't be there to finish by putting out the carved figures.

Gently setting the box down, he took a deep breath and prayed, "Oh God, give me strength to keep going. Somehow." He sighed and squared his shoulders.

Unpacking a hand-carved Nativity, Martin carefully arranged the large painted figures in his store window, just as Katherine had done each and every Christmas for the previous fifty-two years. He positioned the tall figure of Joseph beside the kneeling form of Mary. A shepherd holding a lamb went on the right side. A camel along with three wise men carrying their gifts went on the left.

In the center of the Nativity scene, Martin placed a crude manger along with a baby wrapped in strips of linen cloth, worn from years of use. The old man tenderly touched the baby's tiny hand.

"Ah, Sebastian," he said to his cat, "I wish I could feel the joy of this season. I know I can still give thanks for the birth of my Lord, but Christmas won't ever be the same again. It's just you and me now."

Getting out his long list of holiday orders, Martin looked the paper over carefully and marked a large red X beside the names of all the families with children.

Sounds of laughter from children playing in the freshly fallen snow filtered through the window. The thought of making the children happy sparked a renewed sense of purpose in the old man's heart.

With that he prayed, *Thank You, Lord, for the gift of this store and for over fifty years of work with the people of this village. I want to help these children and be a blessing to them as long as I live. What would I do without their visits?*

The Village Children

"Whoever receives one little child like this in My name receives Me."

MATTHEW 18:5

With his thoughts more focused on the children and Christmas, Martin busied himself with preparations for his daily customers. He searched through shelves and drawers for gift paper in which to wrap the Christmas orders, all the while softly singing the last two lines of "Good King Wenceslas"—his favorite Christmas carol: "Therefore, Christian men, be sure, wealth or rank possessing, You who now will bless the poor shall yourselves find blessing."

Suddenly the doorbells jingled wildly. The front door flew open and a chilly blast of wind and snow blew into the candy shop.

To the old man's delight, a group of children scurried into the store like a flock of little birds. Laughing and talking all at once, the red-cheeked boys and girls crowded around the candy display case.

Joey, the youngest, pressed his worn mittens against the glass case and silently surveyed the wondrous assortment of goodies. Watching Joey's eyes widen while he licked his lips brought a smile to the old man's face.

Times are hard for Joey's family since his father died, thought Martin, noticing the holes in Joey's ragged mittens and coat. *How does his mother manage with six youngsters? I wonder what they do to celebrate Christmas. Hmmm. Perhaps I can help in some way.*

The older boys and girls counted out their pennies and laid them on the counter while they picked out their favorite treats. With renewed energy and a sparkle in his eyes, Martin chatted with the youngsters, packed their candies in brown paper bags, and tied them with red ribbons.

Ben eagerly shared the events of his week. "Guess what, Mr. Winckler. Yesterday I helped pick out a Christmas tree for my family. We'll decorate it tonight and then . . ."

Little Sarah interrupted, wanting to share her own news. "I can't wait to show you the fancy china doll I'm going to get for Christmas," she boasted in a loud voice. "Daddy promised it would be the best he could buy. Nobody will have one like it, I'm sure."

Martin knew that Sarah could only receive such a fine present because her parents owned the village general store. He glanced at the other girls standing silently nearby. *Poor Kristin and Marianna will be lucky to get even one small treat this Christmas,* he thought sadly. *Both of their families will have a hard time making it through the winter. Their bakery needs a lot of rebuilding after the recent fire.*

"Oh, Mr. Winckler," said another boy, grinning from ear to ear. "Did you hear about our Christmas party this Friday? We're going to exchange gifts we've made.

And our mothers are baking fruitcake and fudge and cookies. Lots of cookies!" He rubbed his stomach and licked his lips.

Martin couldn't help but chuckle at the chubby youngster. "Henry, you always love to have fun. And I know you like to eat! I'm sure you will enjoy every minute of this Christmas season."

Suddenly a deep bong echoed from down the street. Hearing the village clock, the oldest boy reminded the others, "It's time to leave. We're supposed to be in our desks in five minutes!"

Martin passed out all the sacks. Then he quickly reached behind the counter and scooped up some of Joey's favorite mints and an assortment of other candy into another bag."

"Wait, Joey." The old man held the bag over the counter. "I have a little gift for you."

The little boy's eyes lit up as he reached for the bag with its prized contents. "For me?" he asked wistfully. "Are you sure?"

"Yes. It's yours, Joey." Martin's eyes clouded with tears. "Merry Christmas to you and your family. I put in extra candy for your brothers and sisters too. I know you're always willing to share."

"Oh! Thank you, Mr. Winckler!" Joey said, heading for the door. The excitement on his face warmed the old man's heart. He watched the youngster run out the door, tightly clutching the sack. Sebastian meowed as a final blast of cold blew into the candy shop. Martin picked him up and held him close while he looked out the front window at the children gathered outside.

"The Lord said it is more blessed to give than it is to receive. You understand that too, don't you, Sebastian? When we make someone else happy, it makes us happy too. Oh, thank You, Lord, for the blessing of being able to give . . . and for renewing the joy in my heart." Sebastian rewarded Martin with a deep rumbling purr and bopped his head affectionately against Martin's chin.

Will They Miss the True Meaning of Christmas?

"Thank you, Mr. Winckler! Merry Christmas!" called the boys and girls. They waved good-bye and raced down the snowy street. Their long knitted scarves flapped wildly in the wind, while powdery clouds of snow swirled upward from their racing feet.

Sebastian meowed again as they watched the children run to school.

"See their excitement, Sebastian. Isn't it wonderful? They're so carefree. Full of

Do not forget to do good and to share, for with such sacrifices God is well pleased.

HEBREWS 13:16

energy and zest for living. Oh, to be young again, eh Tabby?" Glancing upward, the old man smiled and mumbled, "I'm not complaining, Lord. I only wish I had a *little* more zest and youthful vigor in me."

Looking down at the hand-painted set of figurines clustered around the manger, Martin remembered sitting close by his father's workbench many years ago and watching him carve the set. Those were memorable times when they worked together, painting the figures one by one. The many hours of work were intertwined with lengthy discussions as well as stories of God's mercy in the lives of Martin's parents and grandparents.

Now, more than ever, he appreciated having grown up in a home full of faith and love. His parents had witnessed God's loving care, even during difficult seasons of floods, illness, and crop failure. And they had often retold their experiences of God's faithfulness.

What a heritage they shared with me, thought Martin. *A heritage to pass on to my daughter and her family—especially Katie. A heritage to share with the youngsters in this village. They get so excited about holiday parties and presents, but do they know and value the true Gift of Christmas? Oh, Lord, what can I do to help them see? What can I do to show Katie?*

He smiled once more, thinking of Katie. She had the same thick blonde curls and sky-blue eyes as Katherine had enjoyed in her youth. Katie took after her grandmother in so many other ways too—the same exuberance, boundless energy, ability to enjoy every moment, and a heart of love to serve those in need.

"Sebastian, do you remember how my Katherine always prepared such thoughtful gifts for birthdays and holidays?" Martin lowered Sebastian to the floor, and the cat moved toward the back of the candy shop where it was warmer. For a moment, Martin stood lost in thought, remembering how Katherine had always spent weeks making elaborate plans for Christmas celebrations. Every gift would be planned out in great detail . . .

Suddenly Martin realized that he had totally forgotten about the Christmas presents. "Oh, no! Gifts! Sebastian, what will I do? Katherine always took care of what to give others. Now it's up to me. I haven't even given it a thought. Oh, what can I give to Katie?"

He glanced down the street toward the schoolhouse and wondered, *Hmm. What special gift could I give her—and all the other children—as a Christmas surprise?*

He shuffled to the back of his shop and knelt by his worn wooden rocking chair where Sebastian now lay curled up in a ball. "Dear Lord, You know and love Katie and all these children more than I do. How can I help them celebrate the birth of Your Son, the real Gift of Christmas? Show me a way to bless my Katie-girl. Show me a way to bless all Your precious children in this village, especially those who have so little."

With renewed purpose, the old man gripped the chair, pulled himself up, and reached for a handker-chief in his pocket.

"Sebastian, I believe I'm still here for a reason. More work needs to be done." Wiping the tears of joy from his eyes, he added, "Others could use my prayers and my love. Katherine would want me to continue on—right? And God will help me. I know He will."

With a new resolve, Martin stoked up the cooking stove and added some extra wood to warm up the kitchen area. He knew he needed to cook up another batch of candy sticks before the coming holiday week.

Sebastian napped in the rocking chair while Martin placed the heavy kettle on top of the stove. He pulled out the large ceramic jar filled with sugar and measured several cupfuls into the pot. After adding a bottle of corn syrup, he patiently stirred the candy mixture with a wooden spoon and waited for it to boil. When the syrup finally began to bubble, a broad smile broke out on his face. "Aha! What a great idea! Now why haven't I thought of this before?"

What Will It Be?

The old candymaker's eyes brightened as he pondered his new idea. "Thank You, Lord! Maybe that's what I can do! I'll make a new candy—for Katie and for *all* the children—a candy that reveals the real meaning of Christmas."

He laughed at Sebastian, who turned his ears toward Martin without lifting his head. "What do you think, Sebastian? Will it work? What flavor should it be? Vanilla? Almond? Peppermint? Yes! I know Katie likes peppermint."

He shuffled to the cupboard and opened the doors. Squinting to read the labels, he looked over a shelf filled with small brown bottles. Finally he found the one he was searching for. Picking it up carefully, so as not to knock over the other bottles, he shuffled back to the stove and cautiously poured one, two, . . . then three drops into the bubbling pot. Sebastian's head popped up. He sniffed the air with interest.

Martin closed his eyes and took a deep breath of the minty aroma rising from the candy mixture. "Mmm. It smells good. This will remind us of the wise men and their gifts of spices—frankincense and myrrh."

He thought about the angel's message to Mary that very first Christmas.

> *Do not be afraid, Mary, for you have found favor with God. And behold, you will conceive in your womb and bring forth a Son, and shall call His name* JESUS. *He will be great, and will be called the Son of the Highest . . . The Holy Spirit will come upon you, and the power of the Highest will overshadow you; therefore, also, that Holy One who is to be born will be called the Son of God.*
>
> LUKE 1:30-31,35

"All right Sebastian, let's make some white candy, because Jesus Christ is the pure and holy Son of God. And let's make this candy hard—hard like a rock—because Jesus is the solid Rock. He's always there when I need Him. He has never failed me . . . not even now that Katherine has died. And He will sustain me until my life here on earth is finished."

But Sebastian had stopped listening. The room was now toasty warm, and he had drifted into a sound sleep.

Martin patiently finished stirring the syrup, which by now had cooked down into a thick golden mixture. Lifting the cooking pot by its handle, he carefully poured its contents into a large ceramic bowl.

While he waited for the candy to cool, Martin looked around his shop at the vast assortment of sweet treats. Feeling perplexed, he wondered, *Is there any way to make this candy different from ordinary candy sticks? What could I do to make it a reminder of Jesus, the true Gift of Christmas?*

Absentmindedly, he greased his hands with butter, then scooped the warm sticky glob from the bowl and began to stretch it. The more he pulled it, the smoother and the whiter it became. Still feeling frustrated about what exactly he could do with the candy, he continued to pull it vigorously. Over the years, he had prepared countless batches of candy, but today he felt frustrated, unable to think of a new shape to make from the sticky mix.

Lord, I need Your help, he earnestly prayed. *Inspire me! Help me come up with a brand new idea—one that has never been done. A special Christmas gift for Katie and all the children.*

Folding the glob of candy and stretching it one last time, an idea suddenly flashed into his mind.

"Wake up, Sebastian!" His outburst startled the sleeping cat. "I think I've got an idea!" Sebastian opened one eye.

Quickly Martin pulled off a small handful of the pliable mixture and rolled it on the table, using the palms of his hand. The candy glob took on the shape of a long rope. The old man cut off a short piece of the "rope" and slightly curved one of its ends. Smiling, he held up the hooked stick, which reminded him of a shepherd's hook.

"Now doesn't this look interesting? What do you say, Tabby? Now what will Katie and the other children think? I know Katherine would have been delighted." Sebastian yawned, turned around to lie down on his other side, and went back to sleep.

God's Answer!

The dozen copper bells hanging on the front door of the candy shop jingled once again, and a familiar voice interrupted the old man's thoughts.

"Hi, Grandpa! I'm finally here!"

A rosy-cheeked girl with bouncing curls skipped across the room.

Martin turned toward the door with a smile. "Oh, here's my ray of sunshine—precious Katie. What a sweet bundle of energy you are!"

Laying the candy stick on the table, he bent down to kiss the little girl's rosy

Call His name JESUS, *for He will save His people from their sins.*

MATTHEW 1:21

cheek. "Is your kindergarten class over already? My, how the morning hours have flown! Tell me, how is my dearest and most favorite granddaughter?"

She laughed and hugged him tightly. "O Grandpa, you know I'm your *only* granddaughter!"

Martin knew Katie loved her special name, even though she always scolded him when he called her his "favorite" granddaughter.

"I'm so excited about Christmas, Grandpa! Are you coming to our house tonight? You must taste some of the yummy molasses cookies I helped make. Wait 'til you see the way I frosted them and . . ."

She stopped short, spotting the candy stick. "What's this, Grandpa?" she asked, picking up the candy. "Are you making something new? It looks kind of like stick candy, except for the hook. I've never seen one like this before."

Scooping Sebastian from the rocker, Matthew sat down in the creaky chair and leaned back to watch his curious granddaughter. "Tell me . . . what do *you* think it is, Katie?" Sebastian jumped down and went over to Katie. He rubbed against her skirt and purred.

Martin loved the way Katie's tight curls, wet from melting snowflakes, framed her sweet face and her wide, curious eyes. It reminded him of how Katherine looked on the day he realized he was in love with her. A sudden burst of rain had drenched them as they finished the maypole dance. When the storm stopped, the last rays of the setting sun streamed through the clouds in a final burst of light. Sunbeams illuminated all the raindrops clinging to her face, making them look like tiny sparkling stars. What a beautiful sight she was.

Katie's giggle interrupted Martin's thoughts, bringing him back to reality. She turned the candy stick over and announced triumphantly, "I know! It's a cane—like the one you take on your walks, Grandpa."

The old man chuckled at her observation. "Well, I'll be. I didn't even notice that. It does look like my old cane if you hold it on the top."

"And look over there, Grandpa." Katie pointed to the carved figures of the Nativity. "That wooden shepherd is holding a cane too."

"Yes, Katie. You're right again. Actually his cane is called a *staff*. A shepherd uses his staff to comfort his sheep. He rubs the staff across a sheep's back or side—it's a little bit like us giving each other a hug. Sometimes he uses the hooked end to guide sheep along the right path or to keep them from wandering too close to the edge of a cliff. And sometimes the hook is used to pull a lamb away from a poisonous plant or other danger."

He knew she was eager to taste the candy, so he urged her, "Go ahead and see how it tastes. I hope you like it. I made it especially for you, dear girl."

Licking the sweet stick, she nodded her head. "Mmm. It tastes yummy, Grandpa. Peppermint is my favorite flavor."

"Well Katie, you were right about the shape of this candy looking like a shepherd's staff. It can also help remind us of Jesus. Do you know how?"

Katie shook her head, her mouth full of the candy stick.

"Well, Jesus said He was a 'good Shepherd' who loved and cared for His sheep. Do you think a good shepherd would run away from his sheep in times of danger?"

Katie frowned and shook her head.

"No," he agreed. "A *good* shepherd would do anything to save his sheep. He loves them so much that he would willingly give his own life for them."

Katie held up the stick. "I see! Jesus is my good Shepherd, and I'm His lamb." She grinned at her grandpa and added, "And *you* are one of His sheep too."

Martin smiled. He cut off another stick and twisted it like the first. Delighted at Katie's response, he considered how to explain the rest of the meaning of the candy stick.

Turning the newly formed cane upside down, he looked intently at his granddaughter and asked, "What do you see now, dear girl?"

Katie scrutinized the stick. Her eyes popped open with recognition. "Oh! It's a letter of the alphabet! It looks like a J. Why did you make a J, Grandpa?"

"You can think of a good reason. Take a guess."

Enjoying the challenge, Katie surveyed the candy stick. "I can think of lots of J words. Jump and jack and jingle . . . and *Jesus!* Is it a J for Jesus?"

Martin nodded. "Yes. His birthday is the real reason we celebrate Christmas. This new candy J is my special Christmas gift for you, Katie-girl. Do you like it?"

"Yes! Thank you, Grandpa. I love how it tastes!" Katie closed her eyes and wrinkled her nose, breathing deeply. "And it *smells* good too." She paused and looked thoughtfully at the candy. "But . . . there's just one little problem . . ."

Hesitating, she continued, "I do like what you made, Grandpa. But . . . it looks . . . well, it seems kind of plain and ordinary since it is only white. Do you think you could make it look pretty? It needs some color."

Martin nodded as he held Sebastian up to the candy. "Smell it, Sebastian. And take a good look. Katie's right, isn't she? This candy stick is too plain. Well, what can we do about that?" Sebastian sniffed. Then he meowed and looked pointedly at the floor.

After setting the cat down, Martin walked to a cupboard shelf lined with small jars. "I wanted to make the candy J white, Katie, because Jesus is the pure and sinless Son of God. Now let's add some color. Help me, dear girl. What color would you pick? Green? Pink or purple?"

"Use red!" Katie insisted. "Red is the best color for Christmas."

Martin took a jar of food coloring off the shelf and reached into the drawer for a thin paintbrush. "What else does red make you think of?" he asked her.

She watched her grandfather dip his brush into the food coloring. "Red reminds me of hearts. And hugs and kisses . . . and love. Lots of love."

"Ah!" Martin smiled broadly. "You're seeing meanings that I didn't even think of, dear girl."

His brush painted a narrow red swirl around the white staff. When he finished the long stripe, he paused. "The Bible says that God loved the world so much that He gave His one and only Son. Oh, Katie, never forget the very first Christmas gift."

She thought for a moment. "Was Baby Jesus the first gift?"

"Yes," Martin answered. "Jesus was God's greatest gift—a gift of love to the whole world. This red stripe can remind us of God's great love."

Slowly he painted a second red line on the candy stick, rotating the stick carefully as he wound the thin stripe from top to bottom.

"Think again about the color red, Katie," he said in a softer voice. "What else does red remind you of besides hearts and love? Think about Jesus."

"Well . . . He died on the cross. Red is the color of blood," she answered quietly. "The red can remind us of the blood of Jesus."

Neither of them spoke until Martin began painting a third line below the first two. Then Katie asked, "Why are you painting three red stripes, Grandpa? Wouldn't hearts be better?"

"That's a good question, Katie. Stripes can remind us of the wounds Jesus suffered. A whip made stripes across His back. A crown of thorns wounded His head. And nails hurt His hands and feet."

"It makes me sad to think about it," she said.

"Yes, it is sad. But when Jesus willingly died on the cross, He showed how much He loved us, didn't He? So when you taste this sweet candy, think about the sweetness of His love. When you remember the cross, you can also feel glad because Jesus came out of the grave. He's alive! And He's with us today and every day. Those are very good reasons for celebrating!"

Katie squeezed his arm. "Yes, that makes me happy. And someday we'll live with Jesus in Heaven, just like Grandma does."

He paused, looking intently into her clear blue eyes. "Yes, you are right. We will be with Grandma Katherine forever and ever and ever! Heaven is God's gift that will never end. It's a gift you and I don't deserve. We certainly could never earn our way into Heaven. Do you understand, Katie?"

She smiled and nodded.

His eyes glistened as he handed her the finished candy stick. "Here. Now watch how you hold it. It's not quite dry."

Use It,
Dear God!

The chair creaked as Martin rocked back and forth, smiling at the sight of his granddaughter holding the candy stick as it dried. "Well, we did it! I think it's finished. What do you think of this new candy, Katie-girl?"

"I like it, Grandpa! It's a good idea. Now can you make some more? For my friends and to give to my classmates? And what about Joey and his family—could we make some for them?"

"Yes! Yes, of course! Let's work together. I'll roll out each batch and cut them into sticks, then you can curve one end of each stick. You could even try painting them."

His face glowed with joy as he continued, "Let's ask God to show us who needs a gift this Christmas season. I'm sure there are other people who could use a little blessing, like the children who live next to you. Wasn't their father hurt in a woodcutting accident recently?"

Katie nodded. "Yes. We could bring them some candy sticks and a few little gifts. Oh, Grandpa, this will be such fun! I can think of lots of people we could bless. Remember the lame boy across the street? And Julie's grandpa and grandma. Oh—we can't forget Suzanne. She fell on the ice and is home with her leg in a cast. She'd love a special candy stick."

Martin smiled from ear to ear. He enjoyed watching Katie's curls bounce each time she jumped up and down, waving her striped stick. Tears of joy welled up in his eyes while he silently offered up a prayer of gratitude.

Thank You, Lord, for hearing my prayers. You gave me the idea for this special candy. Then You sent Katie to help me expand the meaning of it. And now You're helping us think of others with whom we can share this gift.

A tear ran down the old man's cheek into the stiff hairs of his beard. Clearing his throat, he tried to explain in broken tones. "Katie dear, you don't realize it, but you have been part of God's answer to my prayers today. I wanted to give you a special gift this Christmas, something that represented the real meaning of the holiday. I had a few ideas, but you have helped me see so much more, making it even more special. I couldn't have done it without you. Now that Grandma isn't here . . . well . . . I needed a little extra help."

"It was fun, Grandpa! I like helping you. We did it together. Look how it turned out!" She threw her arms around his neck and hugged him tightly.

"Come, dear girl. Let's kneel down and thank God for helping us."

They laid their candy sticks on the table and knelt on the rug. Martin tenderly wound his arm around his granddaughter while kneeling side by side with Sebastian curled up between them. The old man knew in his heart that he and his granddaughter would always remember this special day.

"How can we thank You, Lord?" prayed Martin. "You have a plan for this candy—a bigger plan than we could imagine. Help us know how to share it with others. Bless all who receive it. Let this candy be a sweet reminder of Your perfect gift of love. May it help people remember the true meaning of Christmas. Amen."

When they got up from the floor, Katie reached for her candy stick. Suddenly she squealed, "Look, Grandpa! Look at our sticks. Do you see how they touch each other?"

"Well, isn't that amazing!" Martin gazed at the sticks whose top and bottom ends connected to form a unique shape.

Katie picked up her candy stick and handed the other one to her grandfather. Silently, they moved their candy sticks closer together until the two sticks touched each other, forming the perfect shape of a heart.

Katie grinned. "We make a great team, don't you think, Grandpa?"

Martin nodded his head, unable to speak as joy flooded his heart. Tears blurred the image of Katie's sweet face and dimpled smile. It was like he was seeing a glimpse of Katherine smiling at him, enjoying this success along with them.

Concerned at his silence, Katie climbed up onto his lap and asked anxiously, "What's the matter, Grandpa? Are you all right? Don't you think we make a good team?" Sebastian hopped up and put his nose in Martin's face. "Meow?"

"Oh yes, yes. Of course. We make the *best* team. I sure needed your help today—it wouldn't have been the same without you!" Hugging her and Sebastian close, he murmured softly, "I thank God for you, my dear little girl." Sebastian licked his cheek. "Yes, you, too, Sebastian."

Then he and Katie laughed.

Outside, the snow fell quietly, covering the little candy store with a soft white blanket. Inside, the warmth of the old wood stove and the sweet smell of candy filled the workshop.

Ever since that special day, the candymaker's unique candy gift has reminded millions of children of the true meaning of Christmas. Little did Martin or Katie know how this little candy stick would become a part of Christmas traditions around the world. Neither of them ever dreamed how God would use the sweet gift that we today call—the *candy cane*.

If you extend your soul to the hungry
And satisfy the afflicted soul,
Then your light shall dawn in the darkness,
And your darkness shall be as the noonday.

ISAIAH 58:10

THE END

Legend of the Christmas Tree

A New Seedling in Shady Woodland

Long ago, say the trees in Shady Woodland, beyond when the elder trees were merely seeds dangling from the branches of their elder trees, sunbeams filtered through towering trees and warmed a little seed that lay on a wooded hillside. Tiny roots broke through the seed casing and burrowed into the earth, deeper and deeper in their search for food and water. It wasn't long before a small green shoot poked through the blanket of pine needles and reached toward the sky.

The LORD does not see as man sees; for man looks at the outward appearance, but the LORD looks at the heart.

1 SAMUEL 16:7

"At last!" exclaimed the new little fir tree, taking a deep breath of the pine-scented air. His tiny branches stretched upward, trying to catch a few scattered rays of sunshine streaming through thick tree branches overhead. He bent backwards and was surprised to see a grandfather fir tree smiling down at him.

"Hi there, little fellow," the grandfather tree said kindly. "Welcome to Shady Woodland. I guess there's always room for one more around here."

In silent awe, the little tree looked up at the towering fir and wondered, *Will I ever grow to be that tall?*

Unfortunately, many evergreens, maples, and elms towered high above the littlest fir tree. And he would soon discover that their branches absorbed most of the summer sun and the fall rain, leaving only a scant amount to ever reach his sparse branches and roots.

He had barely grown a foot when winter arrived. Silent snowflakes swirled from billowy clouds overhead and quietly covered the high branches above the little tree. That night, gusty winds buffeted the branches towering above him. Big piles of snow plopped down on the little tree, bending his branches low. More winds drifted the snowflakes around him until only a few of his tip-top needles could be seen. Hidden under the soft white blanket, the little tree rested his needles. During the long winter months, he thrust his roots deeper and deeper into the dark soil, hoping to grow the next summer as mighty and majestic as the stately trees he so admired.

When the snow finally melted and the air grew warmer, the little tree awoke with a surge of energy. It was time to grow taller. But he couldn't get the sun and water he needed. The other trees got them first.

As season after season passed, the straggly little tree could only stretch upwards a few inches at a time.

Will I ever grow up? he wondered, bending this way and that, straining to catch flickers of sunshine filtering through the pine branches far above him. Feeling more and more hopeless, he realized, *I don't think I'll ever get enough sunlight or water to grow properly.* Two small drops of sap leaked from his trunk in sorrow. "I'll always be small . . . and scruffy-looking . . . and not good for much of anything."

Unfortunately, it was true. And as time passed, the littlest fir tree eventually gave up all his dreams of becoming strong and stately like the other trees of Shady Woodland.

An Important Announcement

The LORD Most
High is awesome;
He is a great
King over all
the earth.

PSALM 47:2

One day, as the golden sun arose at dawn, a loud flapping noise startled the littlest fir tree. He looked up to see a majestic eagle swoop through the highest treetops.

The eagle flapped its wings in graceful rhythm as it loudly screeched, "Be alert! The time is drawing near. Get ready to receive the promised Child, the Son of the King!"

The eagle's announcement echoed across the hillside, stirring up great excitement among all the inhabitants of

Shady Woodland. Trees rustled their leaves with eager anticipation. Animals and birds chattered together, making elaborate plans for this long-awaited event.

The little tree knew something very important was about to happen.

"What's going on?" he called out. He tried raising his voice so the other trees would take notice. "Hello! Will someone please tell me what's happening?"

The forest inhabitants ignored his pleas, far too pre-occupied with their own preparations. Feeling help-less, the littlest tree watched the busy activities with an anxious heart. He couldn't help feeling worried as he pondered the important proclamation. *Who is this promised Child? What can I do for Him?* he wondered.

The older woodland trees murmured and fussed among themselves. They argued continually over who had the finest pine cones, the richest nuts, and the tastiest fruits. The little tree could plainly see that each of them wanted to be the one to give the very *best* gift to the King's Son.

One tall pine announced loudly, "I will give the newborn Child a basket filled with my largest, most perfectly shaped pine cones."

"Just wait until you see my fine fruit," said the apple tree proudly. "These are the most delicious apples anyone could find. Nothing tastes better."

"You're both quite mistaken," declared the pear tree. "I have the best gift of all. Nothing can match *my* sweet juicy fruit."

"Excuse me," said the plum tree. "I don't think any of you understand. My purple plums are the perfect gift for royalty, especially for the *King's* Son."

The grandfather evergreen interrupted them. "Wait a minute, all of you. What does a newborn baby want with pine cones or fruit? A baby only cares for his mother's milk. So I will prepare a gift that will last, one that He can enjoy for many days and years into the future. I will shape my branches into a beautiful wreath that will be the very best gift."

As the woodland trees continued to boast and debate, other forest creatures gave final instructions to their young. "Search for the biggest and the best! Bring your treasures into the storehouse. Select only the best for our King's Son."

Small mice, squirrels, and rabbits scurried around excitedly, while the littlest fir tree watched and listened. "*Who* is this Child?" he asked. "Who is the King?"

None of the animals bothered to answer him as they scampered through the forest, calling to each other, "Gather grain and dried flowers from the meadow! Search out the juiciest figs and huckleberries."

Their cries echoed through the hillside, the orchard, and the olive grove.

"Bring the best seeds from every plant!"

"Select the biggest acorns, pecans, and walnuts!"

"Gather only the finest gifts for the Son of our Creator King." The littlest fir tree had never seen such activity in the forest. *What gift could I give? And what if I can't think of any gift?* The mere thought made his branches shudder from top to bottom. Would he be the only one without a present?

What Gift to Give?

*Praise the
LORD from
the earth . . .
Mountains and
all hills; Fruitful
trees and all
cedars . . .
Creeping things
and flying fowl.*

PSALM 148:7,9-10

In the midst of the hustle and bustle of the gift preparations, a furry-tailed bundle suddenly fell from the branches overhead and landed with a thud near the littlest fir tree.

"Help!" whimpered the young squirrel, lying motionless. "Please help me!"

Preoccupied, all the other animals hurried past without stopping. No one paid any attention to him. Nothing else mattered except the final preparations for the important birth.

The kindhearted little tree spoke up in his cheeriest voice. "I'll help you. Don't worry." Spotting a sleek red fox bounding down the path in search of food, the little tree lowered one of his branches and urged, "Hurry. Climb up and hide among my needles. Do it quickly—danger is near."

Slowly, the injured squirrel limped closer, climbed onto one of the branches, and crouched down near the trunk. As the fox came ever closer, the little tree whispered, "Shhh. Be very still. Nestle quietly in my branches. Relax and stay as long as you want.

The young red squirrel leaned his head against the small but sturdy trunk as the littlest fir tree hummed a lullaby, swayed in the breeze, and rocked him to sleep. It felt good to have a warm, furry bundle snuggled close to his trunk. And it felt even better to know he helped save the youngster from certain death.

Later, when the squirrel woke up, the little tree asked him, "Do you have a gift for the Newborn?"

"Oh, yes!" The squirrel smiled broadly. "My family is going to give Him our finest acorns and walnuts, the very best treasures in our storehouse."

Perplexed, the little tree asked, "Can you tell me *who* this Newborn is who is coming and why everyone is so excited?"

"Well, my daddy said the King of Creation promised long ago to send His Son. Finally, He is coming. He will be born in the village near the bottom of our hillside. He will be a human baby."

"A human baby? But why is He coming? What will He do?"

"Something *very* special," said the squirrel excitedly. "He's going to fix all that has gone wrong on the earth. He will bring us the love of our Creator King. And He will show us a new way to live. Nothing will ever be the same again." Then the young squirrel hopped down and scurried off into the forest.

A shiver rippled through the little tree's branches, all the way down his trunk. What good news! He could hardly wait for the big event.

That night, unable to sleep, the littlest fir tree wondered at it all. Peering through the thick branches overhead, he watched millions of stars sparkling high above the earth. His heart swelled with joy at the thought of the promised Child.

The Son of our Creator King is coming! Is He the One who scattered the stars in the sky? Is He the One who paints the sunset and designs the snowflakes? Did He make everything in the forest . . . even me?

"I want to give the King's Son a worthy gift," he said outloud although no one was listening. "I'm willing to give Him everything I have . . . but . . . ." He paused and thought for a moment. "But what do I have to give?"

Taking a deep breath of night air, pungent with the scent of pine, he thought and thought. *What gift could I give that is worthy of a king?*

Time to Give Gifts

For everyone to
whom much is
given, from
him will much
be required.

LUKE 12:48

Early the next morning, a bright red cardinal landed on a branch of the little tree. The littlest fir tree looked down and said, "Hello there, red bird! Please tell me what *you* will give the King's Son."

The bird cocked his head and smiled proudly. "When the dear Child is born, I will pluck the finest feather from one of my wings and take it to Him. Nothing is too good for the King's Son."

The littlest fir tree sighed. A bright red feather would be a beautiful present. He lifted his thin green branches. Now he was painfully aware of his inability to offer even one small gift.

All too soon the eagle arrived once again, bringing the long-awaited news. "The promised Child has arrived at last. Come to honor Him! Bring your gifts to the place of His birth."

Woodland birds, animals, and trees selected the finest of all they had gathered. Carrying their treasures, they began the happy procession to the village at the bottom of the hill. The little tree's branches bounced with excitement as he moved forward to join the procession.

But he didn't get very far.

"STOP!" The apple tree waved his branches and shouted at him, "Where do you think *you're* going?"

Although he knew he didn't have a gift, the little tree still wanted to go to the village with everyone else. His quivering branches hung low as he stammered softly, "I . . . I just want to . . . to honor the King . . . and His Son."

The apple tree scowled. "It's disgraceful! Unthinkable! Your scrawny branches are completely empty!"

A stately oak, laden with acorns, scoffed at the little tree. "Please! Stay right here where you are. Don't embarrass us by coming. The King would be very displeased."

The little tree's branches drooped. He moved aside, hoping no one else would say anything more to humiliate him. Silently, he watched the birds fly toward the village while other creatures descended the hill with their gifts. He felt awed by the assortment of gifts—elaborate wreaths, huge pine cones, bunches of grapes, stalks of wheat and grain, baskets filled with dripping honeycombs, along with an impressive variety of nuts, fruits, and berries.

The little tree wept silent drops of sap, which rippled down his trunk. He had nothing to give—nothing at all. Sadly, he stared as everyone disappeared out of sight. Standing in the strange silence, the little tree realized he had never felt so alone. Utterly dejected, his branches hunched over and hung down low. Suddenly he was startled by the voice of his young squirrel friend.

"Look! These little ones need help!"

The little tree looked down and saw the young red squirrel pointing at two little mice shivering near his trunk. "Hey there, what's wrong?" the little tree asked kindly. "Can I help you?"

"We're lost!" they sobbed. "We got separated from our mother in the crowd. Now we don't know where to go or what to do. How will we ever find her?"

The little tree smiled and gently wrapped a branch around them. "Don't worry, little ones. You're not lost—you just found me! I'll take you down the hill and I'm sure that together we can find your mother."

Glad for an excuse to follow the other woodland creatures, the little tree's sorrow now turned to anticipation. As he bent his branch low so the mice could climb aboard, he felt his heart swell with happiness about the prospect of helping reunite the little mice with their mother. And he hoped he would get a brief glimpse of the King's Son after all.

Heading down the Hillside

> *"'You shall love the LORD your God with all your heart, with all your soul, with all your strength, and with all your mind,' and 'your neighbor as yourself.'"*
>
> LUKE 10:27

The squirrel moved over to make room for the two young mice who scrambled up the trunk of the littlest fir tree. After each of them grabbed hold of a branch, the little tree straightened up and headed down the hillside path. He knew he would receive an angry response from the other trees when they saw him, but he determined nothing would deter him from his quest.

Partway down the hill, the little tree spotted a mother blue jay hovering above the pathway, fluttering her wings and circling an object on the ground.

"Be careful!" the mother bird shrieked at him. "Watch out for my nest! It slipped off the branch of a giant pine tree, but he wouldn't stop. He wanted to be the first one to see the King's Son. Could you please help me? My precious egg is almost ready to hatch."

"Don't worry," the little tree assured her, carefully edging his branch under the nest. "Come and rest on your egg. I will keep you both safe."

Greatly relieved, the blue jay settled herself on her nest. The littlest fir tree descended the hill, moving more slowly and carefully. He made a great effort to hold his branches steady, so his passengers wouldn't worry about falling off. A warm glow spread out to the tip of each branch. It felt good to be able to care for others in need.

But he couldn't stop worrying about whether he would be able to find the mother mouse. And he couldn't help but dread what might happen when the other trees discovered he had come to see the Child.

It wasn't long before he had a new problem to worry about—the sun was setting.

How would they find their way in the dark? Coming to a split in the pathway, he wondered, *Which path is the right one? If I take the wrong path, we may never arrive at the birthplace of the King's Son.*

"It's no use," he told the others. "I don't know which way to go. We might as well turn back. Soon it will be too dark to go any further."

The mother bird pointed with her wing. "Try the path on the left. The village is in that direction."

So the little tree bravely continued on, barely able to see the narrow pathway in front of him.

Suddenly, strange noises rapidly approached from behind him. He froze in fear. The unfamiliar sounds grew louder and louder. Then a flickering light appeared and the little tree saw shadowy figures of four humans with long sticks in their hands. Their voices sounded excited as they rushed past without noticing them.

"Hurry! We're almost there. Search every stable for our newborn King. Remember what the angel said."

The littlest fir tree trembled with excitement. "We're on the right path!" he told his passengers. "Hang on! I'll go as fast as I can—we must be close."

Arrival at the Birthplace

By the time the littlest fir tree reached the bottom of the hillside, the sun had completely set. Nevertheless, he could still make out the shadowy figures of many of the woodland creatures standing near a stable's entrance at the edge of the village.

The little tree sighed. It would be impossible to see the newborn Child with so many gathered round. Perhaps the darkness would at least prevent the other trees from noticing him as he tried to move closer.

Finally the little tree and his friends reached the gathering. The mother bird whispered, "It's my fault that you're the last one here! I'm so sorry."

In a low voice, the little tree whispered back. "I wasn't supposed to come here at all—I have nothing to give. I just hope I can help the lost mice find their mother. And don't feel bad—I'm glad I could help you."

Now the other trees became aware that he had approached. Scowling, they turned to block him with a wall of their branches.

"Get back!" they warned. "What are you doing here? You have no gift."

The littlest fir tree didn't say a word. It would do no good to try to explain. Hanging his branches down low, he obediently inched backward.

"It's no use," he whispered to his passengers. "We can't get any closer. Now we'll never get to see the King's Son."

Even though he had given up all hope of seeing the Newborn, he didn't want to miss this opportunity to praise his Creator, the King of Heaven. Reverently he bowed his branches, cautious of his precious cargo, and silently prayed.

Oh great King of all, I just want to honor You. I'm so glad Your Son has come. I lift my heart to You, my Creator. Thank You for Your great love. Thank You for sending Your Son to bless the world—to bless me. I'm sorry I have no gift for Him. My thanks and my praise are all I have to offer.

His heart overflowed with joy as he thought about the promised Child. Deep in prayer, the little tree didn't know the King of Heaven was watching him from overhead. He never saw the powerful angel standing near the King's throne. He didn't hear the King give instructions to His angel servant. He didn't see the angel soar high into the sky.

And the little tree never heard the angel call out, "All you stars of the heavens—hearken unto Your Maker! Come quickly to earth and light up the branches of the littlest fir tree. North Wind—come from afar! Blow your frosty crystals over the little tree and make him shine from top to bottom."

A whirlwind surged through the highest heavens, gathering up thousands of stars, and then plummeted toward earth. All the while, the little tree remained oblivious to what was happening. His thoughts were focused completely on the wondrous Gift in the stable.

A blast of the north wind blew the stream of glittering stars toward the little tree. Cascading from the dark blue sky, the stars landed upon every branch of the littlest fir tree. Their bright glow spread as sparkling stars lit up each frosty bough with radiant, shimmering light.

"Ohhh!" cried the mice. "Look, little tree—you're all sparkly and shiny!"

The little tree lifted his scrawny branches and looked at them—each one glowed with bright light. He felt a warmth that penetrated clear to the inside of his trunk.

What is shining so brightly? he wondered. Astonished, he realized that the brilliant display of light emanated from thousands of sparkling stars clustered all over *his* branches!

"Ohhh!" he blurted out. "It's me!"

The other trees and forest creatures turned around and gasped. Speechless, they could only stare at the transformed little tree. His glittering branches glowed with frosty starlight. In awe, the other trees slowly moved back, opening a path to the stable.

Exalting the Humble

Looking into the stable, the littlest fir tree saw a tall man standing beside a beautiful young girl who held the tiny Baby in her arms. Kneeling beside the manger were the shepherds who ran past the little tree on the hillside path.

Slowly and hesitantly, the little tree moved a step forward to get a better look. He felt unsure of what to do or say.

The mother spoke gently to him. "Come closer, little tree," she urged. "You are most welcome here."

"But, but . . . I really shouldn't have come," stammered the little tree. Drooping his branches, he whispered the dreaded words: "I have no gift."

Her warm smile and beckoning hand urged him closer. At last the little tree gazed deeply into the eyes of the sweet baby Boy.

Quietly, the little tree whispered, "Hello, Son of our Most High King. Welcome to the world. I'm . . . I'm so glad You came! I wish I had a gift for You."

With eyes as dark and shining as a clear night sky, the Baby looked sweetly at him and smiled. His two small hands stretched toward the little tree in blessing.

Then a tall shining angel appeared beside the mother and Child.

"Greetings, most honored tree," the angel said. "God the King accepts your thanks and praise. They proceed from the best gift of all—the gift of your heart. Each time you served others, you did what the King's Son has come to do. Now receive your King's blessing. Go in peace. Continue to love and serve your Creator. You will always be remembered for your humble service and your thankful heart."

The littlest fir tree would never forget that moment. Overwhelming joy and peace flooded his whole being. He was loved and accepted by the Creator King! He *did* have a gift to give. He knew his life would never be the same.

The next morning, after the little tree helped the young mice find their mother, he carried the squirrel, along with the mother blue jay and her nest, back up the hill. To his surprise, all the woodland creatures honored him by giving him a wide-open space at the very top of the hill. There he could breathe the fresh morning air, soak in the warm sunshine, enjoy the evening sunsets, and watch the moon and stars at night.

At last the littlest fir tree grew taller and fuller each day. His branches became a favorite nesting place for small birds and animals. All the forest creatures looked up to him and followed the example of his kindness and generosity. They never tired of hearing the story of the time when the littlest fir tree had been covered with stars.

And each year, when Shady Woodland celebrated the birth of the King's Son, thousands of glittering stars in the heavens descended again . . . to light up *the very first Christmas tree.*

> *"The true worshipers will*
> *worship the Father in spirit and truth;*
> *for the Father is seeking such to worship Him."*
>
> JOHN 4:23

THE END

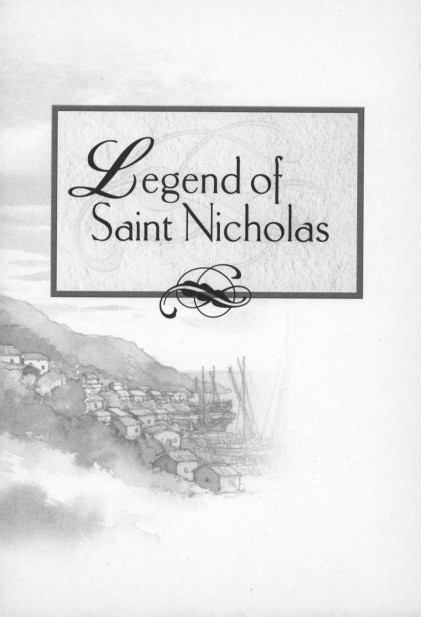

Legend of Saint Nicholas

Life's Changes and Choices

In a time long forgotten, during the reign of the Roman emperor Diocletian, a lonely boy slowly climbed the hill next to a seaside graveyard. With a heavy heart, he sat down beside a cypress tree and looked out over the Mediterranean Sea. The smell of the cool sea breeze mingled with the scent of spring wildflowers growing at his feet. What a stark contrast to the putrid stench in the city! The plague, which had just claimed his two parents, had cut short far too many lives.

Let them who do good, that they be rich in good works, ready to give, willing to share.

1 TIMOTHY 6:18

Deep in thought, Nicholas rested his head against the tree as he scanned the coastline, watching ships set sail and fishermen clean their nets.

How can the rest of the world continue on as if nothing has happened? My world has stopped. Dear Lord, hold my hand. I need You more than ever.

Sadly, Nicholas looked down at the graveyard below where many people stopped by his parents' graves, now just mounds of fresh dirt, to pay their respects to them. It was a comfort to know others loved his parents too.

Tears filled his eyes as he thought back over the previous week, remembering his mother's words.

"Dear son, we prayed many years for a child. Then God gave you to us. What a gift of God you've been these twelve years. Keep serving the Lord. Help those in need. Remember the meaning of your name— Nicholas, "hero of the people." If you remain faithful, God will use you to bless many."

Nicholas could hardly deal with the lonely emptiness of his life. The uncertain future seemed clouded like a ship suddenly enveloped in fog. What would he do at the young age of twelve without his father and mother? After working for many years alongside his parents as they helped widows and orphans, now he, too, was an orphan. How deeply he now felt their pain and, with new eyes, understood their plight.

The approach of someone climbing the hill toward him interrupted his thoughts. The dark wave of hair across the forehead and the stubborn upward lift of the chin told him it was his cousin Karl. Usually the arrival of his cousin heralded a call to action and adventure, but not today.

"Ho, Nicholas! Mother said you should come for supper. And you can stay overnight if you like since your aunt won't arrive until tomorrow."

Nicholas nodded. He didn't like sleeping in an empty house all alone. The emptiness only made the pain worse. He stood up and silently followed Karl down the hill toward town.

When the boys approached the seaport market, three other teenagers joined them.

"Sorry about your folks, Nick," muttered one boy.

"Me too," said another.

"At least you're better off than most people," added the third boy. "Your parents left you plenty of money."

Nicholas couldn't say a word. He didn't care about money. He just wanted his parents. The boys looked

down and kicked the dirt, embarrassed by his discomfort and intense pain.

"Look—oranges!" Suddenly the other boys raced ahead to the market where an elderly woman and a little girl sold oranges out of an old wooden cart.

Helplessly, Nicholas stood and watched the boys grab handfuls of oranges, then kick over the cart. Oranges rolled in every direction. The boys ran back to Nicholas, grabbed his arm, and hustled him into a nearby alley. "Let's stay out of sight for a while. Here, Nicholas—have an orange."

Feeling ill, Nicholas scolded himself. *I should have stopped them. My parents helped that family when the grandfather died.* A twinge of guilt tugged at his heart.

"I'm not hungry," he told the boys. "I'm going back to help pick up the oranges. You ought to pay for the ones you took or ruined."

The boys looked surprised and then laughed. "Oh, who cares? They can pick more. What's the matter with you, Nicholas? We're just having a little fun."

Nicholas felt torn. Needing his friends more than ever, he didn't want the boys to dislike him, but he couldn't treat people like they did. He turned to his cousin and said quietly, "I'll go to your house later."

After Nicholas helped the grandmother retrieve her oranges, he returned home and found a warm woolen shawl that had been his mother's. He wrapped it around one of his family's engraved silver cups in which he placed two gold coins. Then he hurried to a section of town filled with houses in need of many repairs. Tucking the little bundle by the door of the old grandmother's small home, he prayed, "Dear Lord, may these gifts bless this grandmother and child." Then he headed to his cousin's house.

That night Karl came into his room and frowned at Nicholas. "My friends and I don't like how you treat riffraff. You act like they are as good as we are."

Nicholas looked up, his eyes wide with surprise. "Why should how much money people have determine the way we treat them? Aren't we all the same on the inside? Tell me, why are rich people never satisfied? Instead of trying to get more, why don't we use our money to help those in need? Isn't that what God wants us to do?"

Karl reddened at this gentle rebuke and lifted his chin in defiance. He turned his back to Nicholas and went to bed. Unable to sleep, Nicholas knelt beside his bed with his head in his hands.

Givers and Keepers

"Give, and it will be given to you: good measure, pressed down, shaken together, and running over will be put into your bosom."

LUKE 6:38

When his aunt arrived, she assured him, "I know how your parents gave generously to many, including me. If you want to help someone in need, let me know. I'll work with you." Nicholas smiled with relief, hoping she meant those words. He knew his father's relatives rarely understood generosity and kindness given to anyone outside their own family.

Unfortunately, the other relatives did not mirror his aunt's generous attitude. His uncles expected Nicholas to follow in his father's footsteps as a merchant. In the following weeks, they loaded Nicholas's young shoulders with plenty of advice.

"Grow up to be a fine man like your father. Take over his part in our business. But discard any foolish plans of helping those low-class riffraff. They don't deserve it. Remember, God helps those who help themselves."

Nicholas struggled with many decisions during the months ahead. *What should I do? I feel out of place, and I can't fit into other people's plans. I don't like the way they treat the poor and unfortunate.* His unhappiness drove him to his knees. "Direct my path, dear Lord. Help me choose what pleases You."

Karl and his friends brushed off Nicholas's concerns. "We're only young once. Let's make merry while we have the chance." Not understanding his generosity, they ridiculed Nicholas.

Karl sneered, "What's the matter, *Saint* Nick? Are you too *holy* to have a little fun with us?"

Sadly, Nicholas realized, *I don't have even one true friend who understands.*

Discouragement and sadness weighed heavily on him as conflicts with his uncles and his friends increased. They lectured and berated him every time he helped others.

"It's a waste," they told him. "Those paupers will never amount to anything. They'll only take advantage of you."

During the next three years, the struggles in Nicholas's life grew worse. But God answered his prayer and helped him discover new and secret ways of using his inheritance for the benefit of those who were destitute and starving.

One day while Nicholas was riding his white stallion named Alabaster, he saw a fisherman whipping a young boy. Riding up to them, Nicholas inquired, "What's the matter, sir? Is this boy giving you trouble?"

"He is my slave," answered the man angrily. "I paid ten pieces of silver for him, but at the rate he works, I'll never get my money's worth out of him."

"Please sir, would you think of selling him for the same price you paid?"

"Of course," answered the man.

"I'll be right back!" said Nicholas as he quickly turned Alabaster toward home. Arriving at his house, he counted out ten pieces of silver and hurried back to the scene. He handed the bag of silver to the fisherman, who walked off without a word.

"Don't beat me," pleaded the slave boy. "I'll do the best I can for you."

Nicholas laughed. "I didn't buy you to be my slave. I'm giving you back your freedom. Now go home to your family."

"Oh! Thank you! Mother needs me. My father died at sea, and she was forced to give me as payment for the debt he owed."

"Climb up onto my horse," urged Nicholas. "I'll take you home."

A warm friendship grew between fifteen-year-old Nicholas and twelve-year-old Stephen. When Nicholas saw the family's plight, he bought them a small plow and seeds to plant. And he let them use Alabaster to pull their new plow.

His aunt was furious when she heard what had happened. She felt Nicholas gave entirely too much, for though she imagined she was generous, in truth she had a very small heart. "Soon you won't have anything left to give—*you'll* be a pauper like the rest of them!"

At the end of the year, family and friends gathered to celebrate Nicholas's sixteenth birthday. When everyone came to the table, Nicholas told his aunt, "Let's wait to eat until Stephen arrives."

His aunt sniffed and lifted her chin in a way that reminded Nicholas of his cousin Karl. "Stephen won't

be coming . . . he wasn't invited. Surely you understand that he's not one of our kind."

With difficulty, Nicholas remained composed. He had looked forward to Stephen's presence at his party. He smiled a slight smile at the many congratulations from his family and their rich friends. But as soon as he could, he left his party. He went upstairs to his bedroom that night feeling deeply grieved. "I'm trapped in a web with no way to escape. I want to share what I have, but I'm only criticized when I give. My goal is not to gain wealth and possessions. Dear Lord, I want to serve You only—show me how."

After Nicholas had slept for several hours, he suddenly awoke with a start, his mind full of the beauty he'd seen while asleep. He sat up straight in bed and exclaimed, "Dear Lord, is it true? Could this really be so? Surely this is a dream sent by You!" Getting up, he knelt beside his bed, too happy to sleep. The joy kept him there all night.

New Decisions, New Adventures

The next morning Nicholas went immediately to Stephen's house. He told Stephen and his family about the dream: "I saw an amazing place where people worked together and shared everything they had. Think of it! No one was in need because they all gave freely to each other—joyfully and willingly. I feel called to follow that dream. Do you think I might find such a place of selfless giving and sharing?"

Stephen and his family assured Nicholas, "God will lead you and guide you.

Your ears shall hear a word behind you, saying, "This is the way, walk in it," Whenever you turn to the right hand Or whenever you turn to the left.

ISAIAH 30:21

Please take back your horse. You will need Alabaster for your journey. We just sold our harvest of grain, so now we can buy an ox and more seed—thanks to you."

This new decision by Nicholas was not well received by his family, as could be expected. Karl wrinkled his nose as though he smelled something bad and thrust his chin out, "You'll end up as riffraff too. Just like the leeches who follow you!"

But, Karl's disdain could not dim the vision of the dream. Nicholas gave away most of his inheritance to those in need and set out on his new adventure.

During the next two years, he traveled through other countries bordering the Sea. He looked older than a teenager as he grew a beard and let his wavy hair grow longer.

Then one day, at the age of eighteen, Nicholas reined up his horse, felt around inside his empty pouch, and his determination weakened. *Maybe Karl was right.* He slumped down in the saddle and sighed, "What do you think, Alabaster? Was it just an ordinary dream? Is it foolish to believe in a place where people freely give and share all they have?"

Alabaster stood still, waiting. "It's time to abandon my search. It's impossible to go on." The horse plodded slowly forward as though ordered to keep on. Nicholas was too discouraged to stop him. *It doesn't matter where I go anymore,* he thought. And Alabaster plodded on.

Bells rang across the hillside. Going in the direction of the ringing, Nicholas arrived at a small stone chapel nestled on a wooded hillside.

In the dimly lit chapel, he read an open scroll on the altar: *"Ask, and it will be given to you; seek, and you will find; knock and it will be opened to you."*

Nicholas knelt at the altar in a silence that admonished him for despairing too soon. Finally he said, "Yes, Lord. I've been asking and seeking. All right, I'll keep knocking. But . . . what should I do next?"

The smell of fresh-baked bread drifted through a small door standing ajar at the side of the church. Nicholas's stomach growled. Perhaps he could chop some wood in exchange for supper.

The smell of the bread led him to a monastery. The robed baker very generously invited him in. At supper that evening, Nicholas was amazed to find that life

among the monastic brothers was very much like the dream he had had on his sixteenth birthday.

He spread his arms out wide and exclaimed, "I dreamed about a place like this where people shared and worked together. And here you are—sharing all you have, praying together, and caring for the sick and poor in the surrounding villages. This is what I've searched for these past two years!"

So Nicholas became a monk. He happily baked bread for those in need and immersed himself in the monastic life of prayer and worship with his brothers in the faith.

But in less than a year, a day came when a surprised Nicholas felt God directing him to return to Lycia.

Nicholas wondered, *How can I go back to my hometown and help people when I'm penniless? What could I accomplish?*

Nicholas shared his concerns with the head friar who placed a comforting hand on his shoulder. "Nicholas, we are all called to trust God and walk in the path He has destined for us. Remember what happens when one candle is lit in the darkness?"

Nicholas nodded. "Yes. It only takes one small candle to light the room for many people."

"Yes, it does. And others take their light from it and go on, spreading it farther and farther. Who knows how far it may reach? One kind deed can affect many people. It may encourage someone to pray or to give. It may help someone trust God."

Nicholas knew he must accept God's call. So, clothed in a simple monk's robe, he rode back to the province of Lycia.

"In what ways can I serve God's people?" he asked Alabaster. "I can do nothing without God's help. All I have to offer is a heart willing to give and serve. Is that enough, Alabaster?" Hearing his name, Alabaster turned his head and eyed his young master. "You are right to remind me, Alabaster, . . . one small candle." Alabaster turned his head toward Lycia and continued on.

When Nicholas arrived in Lycia, he discovered other Christians already at work helping the poor, caring for the sick, and assisting widows and orphans. With open arms, they welcomed him to join in their service. But first they took him to meet their leader.

When Nicholas saw the young man, he threw his arms open wide and greeted the man with a hug. "Stephen! How you've changed!"

"Is that you, Nicholas? You had no beard when you left!" Stephen laughed. "For over three years, I've wondered if you ever found the place you dreamed about."

Nicholas smiled broadly. "Oh, yes! It's quite a tale how God led me to a brotherhood of men who share all they have. I thought I would stay there the rest of my life, but God has sent me back here. Now I see this fine work you've started among the poor. Would you let me serve God with you and all of your helpers?"

"But Nicholas, *you* started all the work being done here." When Stephen saw the surprised look on Nicholas's face, he explained further. "The gift of freedom you bought for me plus the many gifts you gave me and my family made us able to give to others. You have set hearts in motion, like throwing a pebble into a pond. The ripples have flowed out from me to many others and beyond."

Even though Nicholas was not yet twenty years old, he became a pastoral shepherd to the people of the city of Myra as he prayed for the sick, taught God's Word, and helped poor widows and orphans. At the request of the sailors, he also blessed the ships of those who sailed the sea. Stories of his generosity and kindness began to spread throughout the town, even though he asked the people not to tell.

Stephen smiled at Nicholas's discomfort. "I know you would rather do all your giving in secret," said Stephen. "But it helps us to watch your example. We have learned so much by hearing of your generosity and that of your parents before you."

Soon everyone in the province knew the many ways Nicholas demonstrated his faith and generosity. In spite of his fame, Nicholas remained humble as he continued to give in secret. Now more and more people worked together and helped one another, just as in Nicholas's dream. Indeed, he was living up to the meaning of his name—*hero of the people*.

During this time, a rich merchant in Myra went bankrupt. He was left with no dowry for his three daughters, which was a great disgrace in those days. The father felt he had no choice but to force his daughters into prostitution, so he could obtain a livelihood for the family.

When Nicholas heard about this, he devised a plan to save the girls. Late one night he filled one of his stockings with some of the gold coins given as

offerings for helping the poor. Under the cover of darkness, Nicholas tossed the stocking full of coins through a window of the family's house.

The astonished father used the money as a dowry so his eldest daughter could be married. But he wondered who had been so generous to him and his family. Again Nicholas tossed another sock full of money through the window for the second daughter's dowry. The second daughter married, and still the father did not know whom he could thank for rescuing her.

When Nicholas secretly brought a third sock full of coins, the father had been watching and waiting for his appearance. As Nicholas threw the stocking through the window, the father ran after Nicholas to thank him. Nicholas made the father promise to tell no one while Nicholas still lived.

One day, the elderly bishop of Myra died. He had ruled all the churches of the region of Lycia. Soon, many bishops and priests from other cities and villages in Asia Minor gathered together in Myra to choose his successor.

On the morning of the day the leaders were to choose the new bishop, Nicholas got up very early as usual and went to the church to pray. That morning an elderly priest he'd never seen before was waiting in the dimly lit sanctuary.

"Who are you, my son?" he asked Nicholas.

"I am Nicholas, the servant of Christ Jesus," the young monk replied. Then he bowed low. "And I am your servant."

"Come with me," the old priest directed. He led Nicholas to a room where the other bishops and priests had assembled. The elderly priest explained to all of them, "Last night I had a vision from God that the first person to enter the church this morning should be the new bishop over Myra. Here is that man—his name is Nicholas."

So a surprised Nicholas was appointed bishop. Then, wearing the red robe of a bishop, he became known as the famous "red-robed boy bishop of Myrna."

An Encounter with The Wrath of Rome

One day a Roman official strode boldly into the church where Nicholas knelt in prayer. Hands on his hips, the official lifted his chin proudly and laughed. "Ah, Nicholas. I should have known it was you who joined these "Christ-lings" and organized these troublemakers. You have foolishly angered Diocletian, emperor of Rome."

Nicholas quickly stood up. "Karl—is it you? How good to see you after so many years! But . . . please explain—why would the emperor be angry with me?"

"All the aid you're giving to the riffraff is interfering with our lucrative slave trade here in the province. Now fewer people are being sold into slavery for overdue debts and taxes."

"But Karl, where is your sense of mercy?"

"I have mercy only for the deserving, Nicholas. Now choose—either work with Rome or face her displeasure. If you join us, I'll make sure you regain the wealth you so foolishly gave away."

"I live to serve my Savior, Karl." Nicholas's voice was soft. "There is no greater position than that of a servant."

Stung to the heart by Nicholas's refusal, Karl jutted out his chin, "You'll be sorry, Nicholas!" With this sharp retort, Karl quickly turned and left.

Slowly, Nicholas turned back to the altar and knelt. Once again, he found himself in conflict with his family. He would find out only too soon how his cousin blamed Christians for problems in the empire.

Not many days later, four Roman soldiers entered the church and announced, "You are under arrest by order of Diocletian, emperor of Rome, for inciting rebellion and refusing to comply with the edicts of the emperor."

"Where is your evidence?" asked Nicholas.

"Reports from reliable sources have provided plenty of proof. Now your acts of treason will come to an end!" As the soldiers dragged Nicholas away, he glanced back at the church and saw his cousin, along with another soldier, boarding up the church door.

In the Furnace of Affliction

Nicholas fared even worse in prison than he expected. During the years that followed, Diocletian commanded all imprisoned church leaders to offer sacrifices to the Roman idols. Those who complied went free; those who refused suffered torture.

In jail, Nicholas encouraged the other prisoners with God's Word. "These are the words of life," he told them. "Remember what Jesus said: 'Blessed are you when they revile and persecute you, and say all kinds of evil against you falsely for My sake. Rejoice and be exceedingly glad, for great is your reward in heaven.'"

Even though Roman guards beat and tortured Nicholas and the other Christian prisoners, the believers refused to deny their faith. But many could not help feeling bitter and angry about their plight.

Nicholas spoke out boldly, "Stop your complaints! We must spend time praying for our captors and even for the emperor. God is the only One who can change their hearts."

His fellow prisoners protested. "How can we pray for the pagan Romans? Or for those of our fellow citizens who work for them—they betrayed us!"

"None of us can forgive without God's help," explained Nicholas. "But God will grant us His own mercy and compassion, so we can forgive and pray. And when we pray, God will act."

"What about you, Nicholas?" asked an old man. "Your dark hair and beard are turning white. You'll probably never leave here alive. And it was your own cousin who betrayed you. Do you pray for *him?*"

Nicholas winced. "Yes. It is not easy, but I do. I pray for Karl and the evil leaders of Rome. I remind myself how Jesus loved and forgave those who betrayed Him and crucified Him. Hanging on the cross, He prayed, 'Father, forgive them, for they do not know what they do.' Should this not be our attitude also?" Tears filled Nicholas's eyes. He loved his Lord and wanted to be like Him, but sometimes it was so very hard.

"I have no idea why God has taken me away from the people of Lycia," he continued, "but I have learned to trust Him. I have seen His grace and mercy. I know His hand is still with me in this prison." As they washed each other's wounds, Nicholas prayed with them. "Grant us, dear God, the power to persevere. Help us to forgive those who mistreat us. We ask You to forgive them. Touch their hearts. Help them know Your love."

During the long months and years of their imprisonment, Nicholas led the other prisoners by his example of faith and forgiveness. "Don't give up hope," he urged them. "With God nothing is impossible."

Opportunities for Blessings

Finally, Roman rule changed hands once more, and Constantine became the new emperor. This new emperor used the cross as his symbol and declared tolerance for all Christians. One day a new battalion of Roman guards entered the prison and unlocked the jail cells of all who had been persecuted for their faith. The prisoners cheered in wild unbelief. "Freedom—at last!"

As Nicholas and the other men left their cells, many of the men who had

"Love your enemies, do good, and lend, hoping for nothing in return; and your reward will be great, and you will be sons of the Highest. For He is kind to the unthankful and evil."

LUKE 6:35

worked for Diocletian, including Karl, were brought into the prison and locked up.

One old man angrily shook his fist at the new prisoners. "You pagans! I hope you all rot in here! You deserve to die a miserable death for all our suffering."

"Stop!" Nicholas rebuked him. "It's not for us to judge or curse. Vengeance belongs to the Lord. Our only choice is to love and forgive."

Nicholas knew Karl heard his words, but his cousin looked away in stubborn silence.

Amid great rejoicing, Nicholas returned to his church, which had been reopened and was being repaired. People brought candles and other items from their own households to refurbish the altar.

One young woman brought a beautiful engraved goblet. Nicholas recognized the cup immediately. "Did you ever pick oranges and sell them with your grandmother in the marketplace by the sea?" he asked.

Her eyes widened. "Yes! But how could you know— unless *you* were the secret giver!"

Nicholas's eyes filled with tears as he heard her explain, "We could never bring ourselves to sell this beautiful cup. It always sat on our fireplace mantle as a symbol of God's care and provision."

Also at this time, Nicholas urged his parishioners, "We know all too well what prison life is like. Let's take this opportunity to demonstrate our forgiveness to those who mistreated us. Let us give generously to those former Roman officials who are now imprisoned."

So Nicholas and the others who had spent time in prison sent gifts of food, clothing, and blankets to their betrayers. And when Nicholas learned of the needs of Karl's family, he secretly gave them food and clothing also, thereby sustaining them during the long hard years of Karl's imprisonment.

Rewards and New Beginnings

The years passed. One day Nicholas went to Emperor Constantine with a special request—a plea for the merciful release of Karl, his betrayer.

Your majesty, I entreat you to have mercy upon my cousin and release him from prison," said Nicholas, bent and frail from his suffering in prison. "I have cared for his family during his imprisonment, but they need him."

The emperor objected. "He betrayed you! Think of the years you spent in prison. Think of the pain and misery he caused you."

"God allowed it. And used it all for good in my life. After all, this is what it means to be a Christian. We forgive and show mercy to others like Christ does to us. God wants us to live with a heart of love and forgiveness for all . . . even our enemies."

Not long after this request, Nicholas—hero of the people—died on December 6.

Many people from all walks of life came to the graveside funeral to honor the life of Nicholas. His dear friend Stephen shared an epitaph: "We commit Nicholas, our beloved bishop, into the hands of God. May we continue to follow his example of love and giving. We all experienced his life of faith and his commitment to serve others for the sake of our Lord. As Nicholas gave so often in secret these many years, may the Lord continue to bless and multiply his giving among us."

After the service, a woman and a man with a bowed head slowly approached the grave. In a broken voice, the man told his wife, "Now it is time for us to remember what is most important. Standing here at the grave of my cousin, I know the meaning of God's love

and forgiveness. Every day in prison I was the benefi-
ciary of God's many gifts through the hands of
Nicholas. I only wish I could thank him in person."

"You still can," said his wife. "The best way to thank
him is by following his example of faith."

Kneeling beside the gravestone, the man spoke
softly. "Nicholas, I'm sorry for what I did to you. I
know you've forgiven me. And God has forgiven me
for my pride and arrogance. Thanks to you, I've
changed. I've discovered how it feels to receive a gift
when in need. And I've learned the joy of giving to
others. Now I understand your heart. I want to follow
your example. May God help me."

As Karl stood up, his head still humbly bowed, he
turned to leave. A hand touched his shoulder.

"You don't know me, but I know you," said Stephen.
"Many Christians have prayed for you. We heard of
your release from prison, and we want to welcome you
into our fellowship of believers."

Karl broke down and wept. "Thank you . . . I do
want to join with you."

Stephen grasped Karl's hand. "Come. The others are waiting to meet you."

Together with Karl's wife, they walked away arm in arm. From a view on the hill above, the people leaving the grave looked like ripples of water—ripples created and impacted by a single pebble—the life of Nicholas, the boy-bishop of Myra.

I have fought the good fight,
I have finished the race,
I have kept the faith.

2 TIMOTHY 4:7

THE END

The History of the Candy Cane

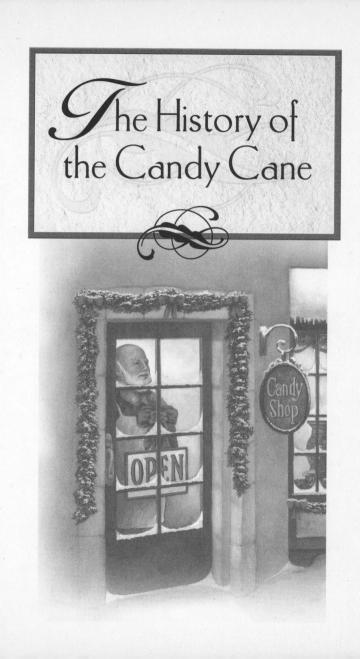

The History of the Candy Cane

A number of stories and legends explain the origin of the candy cane. The most common legend credits the candy cane to a candymaker in Indiana who wanted to make a candy that symbolized his faith. The candymaker's unique design incorporated several elements from Jesus Christ's birth, ministry, and death into the candy.

Another tradition states that the first idea for a candy cane originated over 350 years ago when mothers used white sugar sticks as pacifiers, to calm and quiet their crying babies.

Around 1670, a choirmaster of a cathedral in Cologne, Germany, handed out sugar sticks to his young singers. At Christmas, in honor of the birth of Jesus, the choirmaster bent the sugar sticks at one end, forming the shape of a shepherd's crook. These white candy canes helped keep the children quiet during the long Christmas Eve Nativity service.

From Germany, the use of candy shepherds' staffs spread across Europe, where plays of the Christmas Nativity were often accompanied by gifts of the sweet "shepherds' crooks." Sometimes the sugar staffs were also decorated with small sugar roses.

According to this tradition, candy canes arrived in the United States in the 1850s. A German-Swedish immigrant who lived in Ohio decorated his Christmas spruce tree with paper ornaments and white candy canes. Supposedly, it wasn't until the turn of the next century when red stripes were added to the white canes and peppermint or wintergreen was added for flavor.

No matter what the true origin of the candy cane may be, all the known traditions present a spiritual message. Today we can still share the hidden truths of the candy cane whenever we give them as a reminder of Jesus, the Gift of God that came on that first Christmas. The rich symbolic meaning of the candy cane will always be there for those who have eyes to see and ears to hear.

The History of
the Christmas Tree

The History
of the
Christmas Tree

Evergreen trees, with their changeless color and long-lasting needles, have long been used as symbols of life. However, over one thousand years ago, a monk by the name of Boniface is said to have been the first person to use an evergreen tree to help teach people about God.

Boniface explained that the shape of the evergreen tree, which looks like a triangle from the side view, could help us understand God. Just as a three-sided triangle has three separate lines and corners, so our Lord God is one God, yet made up of three separate and distinct persons—Father, Son, and Holy Spirit.

Some say that Martin Luther was the first person to bring a tree inside his home to celebrate Christmas. One clear frosty night, as he walked home through the woods after a Christmas Eve church service, it appeared that thousands of twinkling lights were lighting up the trees. It turned out that what looked like lights was actually starlight reflecting off tiny icicles hanging from the evergreen branches and needles.

So Martin Luther cut down a small evergreen and took it home to his family. He set it up in his living room as a reminder of the living presence of Jesus among us. Martin Luther also is credited with using small candles on the tree's branches as a reminder of Jesus Christ being the light of the world.

Later, as more people celebrated the birth of Christ, they often decorated evergreen trees with glass ornaments and trinkets or sweet treats such as breads, candy, and cookies. Many other symbolic ornaments were added as reminders of the Christmas star, the angels, and the shepherds' lambs.

The History of
Saint Nicholas

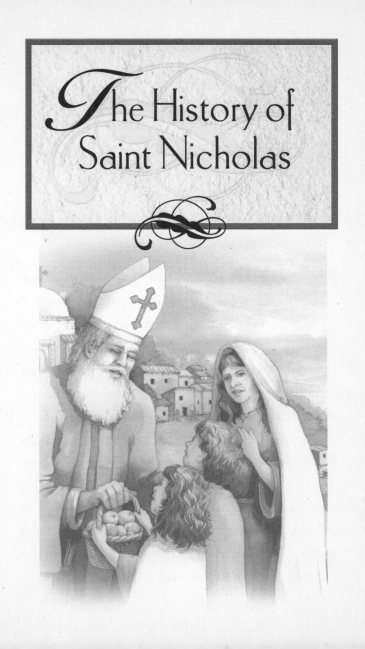

The History of Saint Nicholas

Countless legends abound regarding Saint Nicholas, but few historical facts are known. He was born the only child of wealthy parents in the city of Patara, about A.D. 270-280. Today this area is part of the country of Turkey. Nicholas's parents were devout Christians who used their wealth to perform many deeds of kindness. They died in the plague, which was rampant in Europe during the late third century, leaving Nicholas an orphan at a young age.

Stories about Nicholas's generosity and secret giving grew into great legends. It is known that, at the age of nineteen, the bishops of Asia Minor elected Nicholas as bishop over Myra in the province of Lycia. He was known as a generous and kind man of faith.

From 284-305, Diocletian ruled as emperor of Rome over the areas of Turkey and Eastern Europe. He burned many churches and ordered a brutal persecution of all Christians, attempting to force them to sacrifice to pagan gods. Nicholas and others who refused were tortured and killed or imprisoned during this great persecution.

After many years of imprisonment, Bishop Nicholas was freed by decree of the new emperor who had become a Christian—Constantine the Great (313-337). People welcomed their beloved Nicholas back to Myra with open arms where he served for another thirty years, wearing the red robe of a bishop.

Nicholas's death is recorded as December 6, however the year varies in his biographies (between A.D. 343 and 352). He was buried in his cathedral. In 1087, when the city of Myra fell into the hands of the Saracens, his remains were taken to Bari, Italy, where a new church was built to house his tomb. To this day, Saint Nicholas continues to be the patron saint of sailors as well as little children. Church symbols for Saint Nicholas include a bishop's crosier, three money bags, and a ship's anchor.

About the Author

Helen Haidle, winner of the 1997 Mount Hermon Pacesetter Award, is a beloved author of over thirty-five books for children of all ages. After college, she served as director of Christian education of congregations in Worthington, Minnesota; Spokane, Washington; and Beaverton, Oregon. She has worked with Sunday school teachers, women's Bible study groups, youth groups, and children's ministries.

Her first published work came out in 1989: *He Is My Shepherd,* an illustrated book on the Twenty-third Psalm. With artwork by her husband David, this book won the 1989 C. S. Lewis Silver Award.

Helen's first fiction illustrated book, *The Candymaker's Gift,* has sold over 160,000 copies. It received both a 1997 Gold Medallion nomination and the 1997 C. S. Lewis Silver Award.

Helen's books have sold over 1,400,000 copies. CBA bestsellers include *He Is Alive, What Did Jesus Promise?, A Pocketful of Promises, A Pocketful of Proverbs, God Made Me, What Would Jesus Do?, What Would Jesus Do* (board book), and *The Candymaker's Gift.* Three of these books also received Gold Medallion nominations.

Helen's husband, David, has illustrated twelve of her books. The Haidles live and work in their home studio at the edge of the Deschutes National Forest in the Oregon Cascade Mountains.